NATURAL WORLD

ELEPHANT

HABITATS • LIFE CYCLES • FOOD CHAINS • THREATS

Will Travers

RAINTREE
STECK-VAUGHN
RSVP PUBLISHERS

A Harcourt Company

Austin   New York
www.raintreesteckvaughn.com

NATURAL WORLD

Chimpanzee • Elephant • Giant Panda • Great White Shark
Killer Whale • Lion • Polar Bear • Tiger

Cover: An elephant raises its trunk to sniff the air.
Title page: A young calf
Contents page: A large male elephant
Index page: Elephants having a dust bath

Published by Raintree Steck-Vaughn Publishers, an imprint of Steck-Vaughn Company

Library of Congress Cataloging-in-Publication Data
Travers, Will.
Elephant / Will Travers.
    p.   cm.—(Natural world)
    Includes bibliographical references and index.
    Summary: Explains the physical characteristics, life cycle, habits, and habitat of the elephant.
    ISBN 0-7398-1056-1 (hard)
    0-7398-0947-4 (soft)
    1.Elephants—Juvenile literature.
    [1. Elephants.]
    I. Title. II. Series.
    QL737.P98T725 1999
    599.67—dc21   98-53266

Printed in Italy. Bound in the United States.
  2 3 4 5 6 7 8 9 0 04 03

Picture acknowledgments
Born Free Foundation back cover; *Bruce Coleman Collection:* 1 Michael Freeman; 6 Werner Layer; 7 Hans Reinhard; 9, 11, 13, 28, 33, 37, 39, 44t, 44b M P Kahl; 10, 31, 44m John Shaw; 15 Christian Zuber; 16 Eckart Pott; 18 Gerald Cubitt; 19 Leonard Lee Rue; 20 Atelier G&M Kohler; 21 Sophy and Michael Day; 24 Eckart Pott; 26, 36 Johnny Johnson; 29 Andy Price; 30–31 Gunter Zeiesler; 32, 48 Christer Fredriksson; 34, 45t Jen & Des Bartlett; 38, 40 Gerald Cubitt; 42 Mark Boulton; 43 Peter Davey; *Digital Vision* 3, 8, 12, 22, 25, 27, 35, 45m, 45b; *Still Pictures* front cover, 14, 23 M&C Denis Huot; 40–41 Alain Compost. Artwork by Michael Posen.

Contents

Meet the Elephant

Elephants are the largest land animals in the world. They are very strong, are extremely intelligent, and have remarkable memories.

Unlike most animals, elephants continue to grow throughout their lives—the older they get, the bigger and more impressive they are.

Trunk
An elephant's trunk is made up of 100,000 muscles and no bones. It is very flexible and can be used to push, pull, and pick up objects, put food in the elephant's mouth, suck up water, and make sounds.

Ears
An elephant's huge ears help it keep cool.

ELEPHANT FACTS

Elephants can live to between sixty and seventy years old.

•

Male elephants are known as bulls, females as cows, and infants as calves. They live in close family groups.

•

Elephants' trunks can grow to over 6 ft. (1.8 m) long.

•

The longest recorded tusk measured 11.3 ft. (3.45 m), and the heaviest pair of tusks weighed 516 lbs. (234 kg).

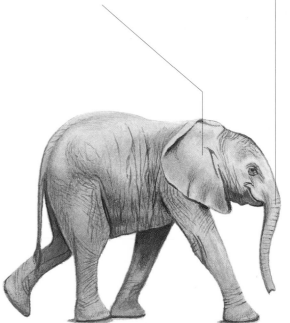

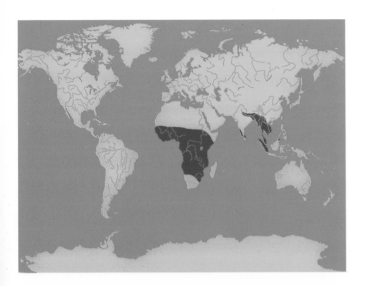

 Elephants live in many different habitats, including savannahs, rain forests, swamps, and mountains.

Key to map

African elephants

Asian elephants

Tusks
Tusks are actually huge incisor teeth. Elephants use them to dig for water and to strip the bark from trees.

▼ A female African elephant and her calf

Skin
Elephants have very sensitive skin. They often wallow in mud to protect their skin from the sun and from insects.

Teeth
Elephants have six sets of molar teeth for grinding up their food. When a front tooth wears out, another moves forward to take its place.

Elephants are unlike any other animals alive today. Their closest living relatives include hyraxes (large, guinea-piglike animals) and sea cows (marine animals that feed on plants).

There are two species of elephants. They are the Asian elephant (*Elephas maximus*) and the African elephant (*Loxodonta africana*). They may look very similar, but there are important differences.

African elephants weigh between 4 and 7 tons, whereas Asian elephants weigh from 3 to 5 tons. At up to 13 ft. (4 m) high, the African elephant is also much taller than the Asian elephant.

▼ It is difficult to believe that this rock hyrax is a relative of the elephant.

▲ The back of an Asian elephant, like this one, is flat or slopes down, while an African elephant's back dips in the middle.

The tusks of an African elephant are bigger than those of the Asian elephant, and its ears are also bigger. African elephants normally have rougher, more wrinkled skin than Asian elephants. This book will tell you about the life cycle of the African elephant.

An Elephant Is Born

As darkness falls, a female elephant moves heavily away from the herd. Inside her, a calf has been growing for nearly two years, and she is ready to give birth. In the shadows, another female quietly joins her. She will stay with the mother during the birth.

Elephant cows give birth to one calf every four years or so. Twins are rare. Within half an hour of being born, the calf can stand up. Then it moves on wobbly, unsure feet to find safety underneath the belly of its mother. Close by, the second female elephant stands guard. Soon, the calf begins to suckle on its mother's rich milk.

▶ This calf is trying to suckle its mother's milk.

▼ A female elephant prepares to give birth. Her companion will give her support during the night.

8

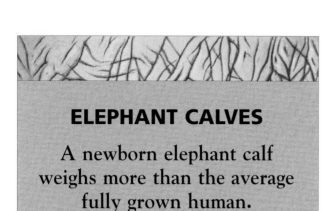

ELEPHANT CALVES

A newborn elephant calf weighs more than the average fully grown human.

●

Female calves weigh up to 220 lbs.(100 kg), and males weigh up to 265 lbs. (120 kg).

Dawn breaks and the chorus of birds is drowned out by the trumpets, squeals, and rumbles of the elephant family as they greet the new calf. There is great excitement as, one after another, they touch and smell the tiny calf with their trunks.

▲ This tiny calf seeks shelter under its mother's belly.

◀ Within two days of being born, the calf can keep up with the family group as it travels in search of food.

Staying Safe

The calf needs the reassurance and protection of its mother. For the first two months, it stays very close to her.

Calves in the same family group are often born together at about the same time of year. This allows mothers to share the job of looking after the calves and means the young have companions to play with.

11

Growing Up

In its first few months, the young elephant learns a great deal from its mother and the other family members. They teach it what to eat and where to find food, water, and mud-wallows. The calf also starts to learn how to behave with other elephants—how to play, greet, and communicate with them and how to protect itself.

▲ As a young calf grows, it learns by watching the other elephants.

DRINKING MILK

During its first two years or so, a calf will drink about 7 gal. (28 l) of its mother's milk a day.

●

It can gain up to 45 lbs. (20 kg) a month.

As the calf gets older, it begins to wander farther from its mother and explore its surroundings. At this time the other females play an important part in caring for the calf. This gives them valuable practice for the future when they become mothers. It also increases the calf's chances of surviving.

▶ This calf is just starting to eat grass like the adults, but it continues to suckle its mother's milk until the age of six.

Fun and Games

By six months old, the calf has become lively and
playful. Although never far from its mother, the
calf explores and becomes more confident. Since
the calf still feeds on its mother's milk and
doesn't have to spend all day finding food,
it has time to play with others of its own age.

▲ Playing is a good
way for the calf to
learn about its
surroundings.

The young calves spend their time racing around, sometimes picking up tree branches and twirling them around with their trunks. They show their joy by trumpeting, roaring, and flapping their ears. A favorite game involves charging at birds, such as the beautiful white cattle egrets that stalk through the grass eating insects disturbed by the elephants' feet.

▼ Calves of a similar age often play together.

What Elephants Eat

By the time it is six years old, the young elephant has stopped drinking its mother's milk and is eating the same food as the adults. Deep in the forest, it watches the older and bigger elephants use their great strength to push over bushes and trees, bringing the new leaves on the highest branches down to within reach.

Elephants spend up to eighteen hours a day feeding. They use their trunks to pick up the food and put it in their mouths. Then their large molar teeth grind up the food.

▼ Elephants mostly eat grass, but their diet also includes a wide variety of roots, leaves, bushes, bark, and fruit.

ELEPHANTS' APPETITES

Not surprisingly, elephants have big appetites. An adult elephant eats up to 500 lbs. (230 kg) of food every day.

●

An elephant can digest only about 40 percent of what it eats. The rest is plant matter that is returned to the earth as dung.

▼ Healthy adult elephants have no natural predators, but lions and crocodiles will attack calves. (The illustration is not to scale.)

ELEPHANT FOOD CHAIN

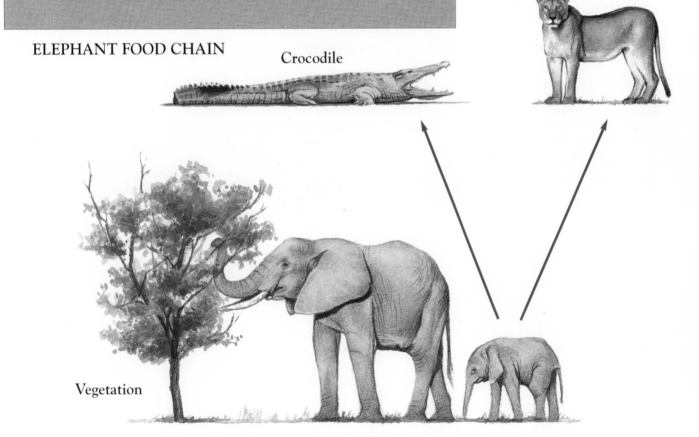

Crocodile

Lion

Vegetation

Sometimes elephants will eat particular soils that are rich in salts and other minerals that their bodies need. Adult elephants can drink more than 53 gal. (200 l) of water a day—this would fill more than 600 soda cans.

Life in the Herd

The mother and her calf live in a family group led by an older female, called the matriarch, who may be sixty years old. The family group is made up of four generations—the matriarch and her sisters, their daughters, granddaughters, and great granddaughters.

▼ Family groups usually consist of about eight elephants, but they can be larger.

▲ Young males play-fight, in practice for the contests of strength they will face when they are older.

The father of the calf does not live within the herd. Males usually live on their own or together in "bachelor" groups.

As a female calf grows older, she will spend more and more time "mothering" the younger calves in her family group. She will learn to look after them, preparing for the time when she has her own calf.

▲ Elephants drink by filling their trunks with water and squirting it down their throats.

At the Waterhole

In hot, dry weather, the elephants' skin feels itchy and uncomfortable. Flies buzz around annoyingly. The herd moves across the plain to the waterhole. The elephants wade out into the deeper water, splashing excitedly and throwing mounds of rich mud over their backs.

At a waterhole, elephants drink, bathe, and spray themselves with mud. Elephants have very sensitive skin, even though it can be more than 1.5 in. (3.8 cm) thick in some places. The mud helps protect their skin from the hot sun and from insect bites. Elephants also spray dust over themselves to care for their skin.

◄ An elephant uses its trunk to spray mud across its back.

Few other animals are powerful enough to attack a healthy adult elephant. But a big cat, such as a lion, may kill an elephant calf, especially if it is caught off guard when it is busy feeding. The elephants' excellent hearing makes up for their poor eyesight. As soon as they detect danger, they surround their young to protect them.

Elephants have the biggest ears in the world. In each ear, there are millions of tiny blood vessels just under the skin. When an elephant flaps its ears, the breeze cools the blood and helps the elephant stay cool.

▶ To scare off a lion, elephants fan out their ears and make loud trumpeting calls.

▼ A pride of lions may try to prey on a small elephant calf.

Elephants and the Environment

Elephants can completely change the look of an area of forest or grassland in just one night of eating. They knock over trees and bushes and leave broken vegetation strewn over the ground. As they trundle through the dense forest in search of food, elephants create pathways through the vegetation.

▼ This elephant is chewing the bark off a damaged tree.

The effect that elephants have on the environment is not necessarily bad. The elephants are changing their habitat rather than destroying it.

When elephants knock over trees and bushes, they let light into an area, which allows grasses to grow. This can help break up the soil, which may lead to the creation of waterholes. Antelopes and other animals can then move into the area because there is food and water for them to live on.

▲ Antelopes and other animals benefit from the ways in which elephants change their habitat.

Sometimes an elephant family meets up with other family groups. When two groups meet, the elephants greet each other by touching trunks, trumpeting, and rumbling. They spend some time together before going their separate ways again.

An elephant could not survive without its amazing trunk. It is sensitive enough to pick up a small fruit and strong enough to lift a massive log. Elephants also use their trunks to push, pull, suck, sniff, blast air, and to make noises.

▲ Elephants do not have a fixed territory. They travel across vast areas of land in search of food and water.

► Elephants can stretch out their trunks to reach food high in the trees.

▲ These elephants are traveling in search of food during a time of drought.

Hunger and Thirst

In long periods of hot, dry weather, many trees and bushes become brown and scorched. Then elephants have to travel long distances in search of food.

Many waterholes dry up. Using their tusks, the elephants will dig underneath a dried-up riverbed to try to find water.

WHEN ELEPHANTS DIE

Sometimes a large number of elephant bones are found in one place. People used to believe that these were "elephant graveyards." This is not true. Elephants die wherever their herd is at the time.

•

Elephants can recognize the bones of other elephants. If an elephant finds the bones of a dead elephant, it may touch them with its trunk and pick them up.

Sometimes an elephant will not be able to make the long journey. Weakened by lack of food and water, an elephant may become so tired that it cannot keep up with the herd. Then the other elephants support it. Two strong elephants place themselves on each side to hold up the weaker one. But eventually, if the tired elephant becomes sick, it can take no more and falls down to die.

▼ This waterhole is nearly empty, but every drop is precious when supplies are low.

If a sick elephant has a calf, the other females in the herd may adopt the calf and take turns looking after it.

Adult Life

By the age of twelve, a young female elephant is mature. She will stay among her mother's family group to have her young. She will probably have her first calf when she is about fourteen or fifteen years old.

▼ Two young adult males enjoy themselves at a waterhole.

▶ Males spend most of their time testing each other's strength. They lock tusks and grapple with their trunks.

Life for a bull elephant is very different. He will stay with the family group until he is about twelve to fourteen years old. He may then join a group of other males until he is old enough to breed—about thirty.

Although younger bull elephants spend a lot of time with older bulls and probably learn from them, they do not form the strong family relationships that the females do.

ELEPHANTS' TUSKS

Tusks are made of ivory, (like human teeth) which is a special mixture of dentine and other substances. An elephant's tusks grow by as much as 7 in. (17 cm) a year.

•

Both male and female African elephants have tusks. Male Asian elephants have large tusks, but females have tiny tusks or no tusks.

As a bull elephant becomes mature, he spends more time on his own. He competes with other elephants to become the dominant bull in the group. The dominant bull has the best chance to mate with the cow elephants.

Often the bull elephants with the largest tusks are the strongest fighters. They will fight for up to six hours over who is going to mate with a particular cow, and their battles can become quite violent.

◀ This male elephant has grown a fine pair of tusks.

▼ When a bull elephant is aggressive, a thick fluid flows from glands between its ears and eyes.

Once a bull reaches about twenty-five years of age, he goes through a period of change once a year. This is a period when elephants behave in a very aggressive and frightening way. The bulls stride around, searching for females to mate with and fighting with other bull elephants they meet. Most bulls will avoid other bulls during this time. Cow elephants prefer to mate with bull elephants that are aggressive.

A female elephant can have young when she is about fourteen years old. But first she must attract a male with which to mate.

▼ A female elephant usually has from four to six calves during her lifetime.

Because the bulls do not live within their family groups, the females let the male know that they are ready to mate by using scent and sounds. Once the males are close enough to see them, body language shows them that the females are ready to mate.

▲ Bull elephants do not help care for their calves.

When they have mated, the bull leaves. During the twenty-two months that the cow is pregnant, she is looked after by the other females in her herd. Once she has had a calf, it is usually up to a year before she can become pregnant again.

The Memory of an Elephant

Elephants can live sixty to seventy years. The leader of the herd, the matriarch, holds a very special position. She has great knowledge, which she has learned over many years, through her own experience and from her mother and the other females in the group.

Elephants have excellent memories. The matriarch's memories of past places and experiences probably help her know where to go to find food, how to reach water in times of drought, how to avoid predators such as lions, and how to keep the family safe.

▼ The matriarch is responsible for the safety of her family group. She is throwing dust as a warning.

36

Growing Old

Elephants have six sets of molars that they use to grind up their food. Throughout an elephant's life, as the teeth at the front of the jaws become worn out, they are replaced by others that move forward from behind. When the last of the six sets of molars has worn out, the elephant is unable to eat as much food as it needs. Eventually, it dies.

▲ Many elephants die of malnutrition when they grow old. But most, like this one, are shot by hunters before they get old.

Threats

The biggest threat to elephants is the trade in ivory, which comes from their tusks. In the past, ivory was used as a kind of currency, and more recently it has been used to make billiard balls, piano keys, and ornaments. In Japan, ivory is made into signature stamps called *hankos*.

▼ An antipoaching unit in Kenya inspects a pile of elephant tusks taken by poachers.

38

▲ This female was
wounded by poachers.

Ivory can be taken only from dead elephants. Since ivory commands a very high price, many elephants have been killed illegally by poachers, who shoot them and saw off their tusks.

In the 1970s and 1980s, the growth in the ivory trade began to drive the elephant to extinction. Between 1970 and 1998, the number of African elephants fell from two million to 400,000. The Asian elephant's numbers have also fallen. There were about 100,000 in 1900, but today only 35,000 to 50,000 are left in the wild.

In 1989, trading in ivory was banned all over the world. In the following years, elephant populations in some countries stopped falling. In a few cases, elephant numbers began to rise.

◄ This armed patrol is on the lookout for elephant poachers.

ASIAN ELEPHANTS UNDER THREAT

In the countries where Asian elephants live, the number of people is growing rapidly, and less room is left for elephants.

●

Elephants are taken from the wild and trained to work in the forests, to take part in ceremonies, and to take tourists on elephant rides. The training is often very cruel.

●

Like African elephants, Asian elephants are killed for their ivory.

However, in 1997, a world conference decided to allow ivory trading to start again. The conference hoped that the trade would be strictly controlled and that illegal poaching would be stopped. Many conservationists and wildlife protection organizations don't believe that poaching will stop.

▼ These Asian elephants have been trained to move heavy logs in the forests of Indonesia.

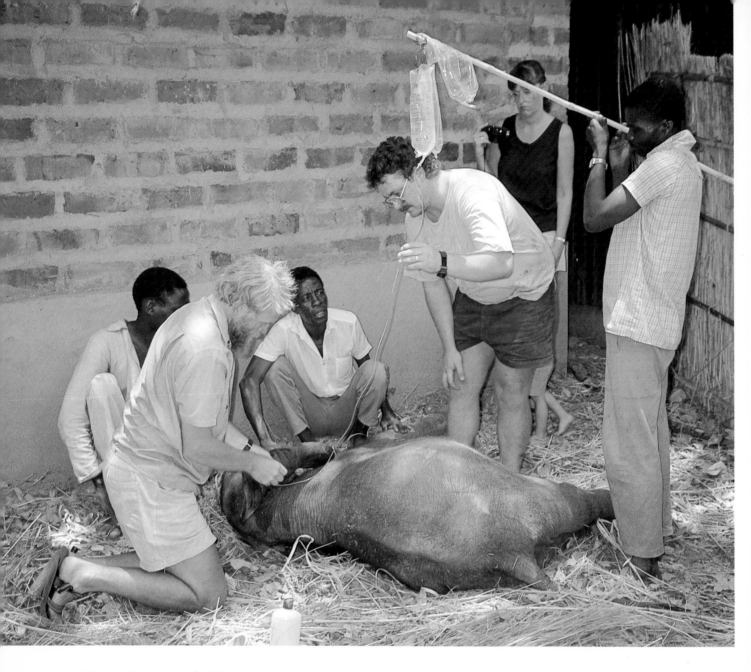

Not Enough Room

Another great threat to the elephant comes from the increasing numbers of people in the world. More people need more land for houses, farms, roads, and factories, and less space is left for elephants and other wildlife. Hungry elephants will raid farmers' fields. While farmers protect their crops, the farmers, the elephants, or both can get hurt or even be killed.

▲ This rescued orphan elephant is being cared for. Rescued calves can be returned to the wild.

The elephant's future is in our hands. Many wildlife protection organizations are working hard to save the elephant by educating people about the important place this amazing animal has in the wild.

▼ Many elephants can find safety in big national parks and preserves, such as Samburu in Kenya.

They are also trying to find ways for people and elephants to live in harmony. You can help by joining one of these groups and becoming involved in the elephant's future. A list of addresses is included on page 47.

Elephant Life Cycle

 1 Usually just one calf is born about twenty-two months after the cow elephant has mated with the bull. The calf can walk within about half an hour and is suckling from its mother shortly afterward.

 2 For the first two months, the mother keeps her calf close by her all the time.

3 From the time that it is just a few months old, the calf travels around with the elephant herd and begins to eat small plants and grasses. Yet it will probably continue to drink its mother's milk until it is about six years old.

4 ▷ At around twelve to fourteen years of age, female elephants are usually ready to mate with bull elephants.

5 ▷ An elephant is considered to be mature when it reaches the age of twenty-five years. By this time the bull elephants are living outside the herd, but the cow elephants will remain within the herd for their entire lives.

6 ▷ Elephants can live to be around sixty to seventy years old.

Glossary

Body language Communicating by using body movements rather than sounds.

Dominant A word describing the lead animal in its herd or group.

Drought A long period when there is not enough rain.

Incisors Teeth at the front of the jaw. Your two large front teeth are incisors, and so are an elephant's tusks.

Ivory The hard, white substance that makes up most of the tusks of elephants.

Malnutrition Not having enough food or the right kind of food to eat.

Matriarch The female leader of a family group or tribe.

Mature Grown up.

Molars Large teeth, often at the sides of the jaw, used for grinding food.

Orphan A child or young animal whose parent or parents are dead. An elephant calf becomes an orphan when its mother dies.

Poachers People who hunt and kill wild animals illegally.

Predators Animals that kill other creatures for food.

Savannah Open grasslands, usually with scattered bushes or trees.

Suckle To give or take milk from a mother's teats.

Territory The area that is controlled and defended by an animal.

Waterhole A pond or pool where animals go to drink.

Further Information

Organizations to Contact

Earth Living Foundation
P.O. Box 188
Hesperus, CO 81326
(970) 385-5500

Friends of the Earth
1025 Vermont Avenue NW
Suite 300
Washington, D.C. 20005-6303
(202) 783-7400

Survival International
11–15 Emerald Street
London WC1N 3QL
Tel: 0171 242 1441

World Wildlife Fund
1250 24th Street NW
P.O. Box 96555
Washington, D.C. 20077-7795

Web Sites

The Elephant Sanctuary
www.elephants.com
A refuge in the U.S. for sick, old, and endangered Asian elephants.

The Elephant Information Repository
http://elephant elehost,com/
Information, news and links.

Books to Read

Dudley, Karen. *Elephant* (Untamed World). Austin, TX: Raintree Steck-Vaughn, 1997.

Grace, Eric S. *Elephant* (Sierra Club Wildlife Library). Boston: Little Brown, 1996.

Patent, Dorothy Hinshaw. *African Elephants: Giants of the Land.* New York: Holiday House, 1991.

Pringle, Laurence. *Elephant Woman: Cynthia Moss Explores the World of Elephants.* New York: Atheneum Books for Young Readers, 1997.

Redmond, Ian. *Elephant* (Eyewitness). New York: Knopf Books for Young Readers, 1993.

Travers, Will. *The Elephant Truck* (Born Free Wildlife). Ridgefield, CT: Millbrook Press, 1998.

Index

All the numbers in **bold** refer to photos and illustrations.